WHEN ESCAPE BECOMES THE ONLY LOVER

Poems

Tendai Rinos Mwanaka

Typeset by Tendai Rinos Mwanaka
Cover: **When escape becomes the only lover** © **Tendai Rinos Mwanaka**

Mwanaka Media and Publishing Pvt Ltd,
Chitungwiza Zimbabwe
*
Creativity, Wisdom and Beauty

Publisher: Tendai R Mwanaka

Mwanaka Media and Publishing Pvt Ltd *(Mmap)*

24 Svosve Road, Zengeza 1

Chitungwiza Zimbabwe

mwanaka@yahoo.com

www.africanbookscollective.com/publishers/mwanaka-media-and-publishing

https://facebook.com/MwanakaMedia.AndPublishing/

Distributed in and outside N. America by African Books Collective

orders@africanbookscollective.com

www.africanbookscollective.com

ISBN: 978-1-77906-492-9

EAN: 9781779064929

DISCLAIMER

All views expressed in this publication are those of the author and do not necessarily reflect the views of *Mmap*.

Table of Contents

Introduction

This collection, as I noted in the introduction of *A Portfolio of Defiance* (2013-2014), could be taken as a continuation and a crowning moment of this series of 4 poetry collections I wrote between 2009-2016, the other ones are *Logbook Written by a Drifter* (2009-2010), and *Revolution: Struggle Poems* (2011-2012). Continuing from where I left off in *A Portrait of Defiance* this collection still investigates the poetic agency and voice, especially human voice in the poem *Running towards the Song I Will Never Hear, It Takes Hell, To a Text Maker Who Leaves Nothing to Chance.*

There is still that irreverently zestful playing around with number poetry in the poem, *A text for Baga* and in *Is this the "next Rwanda?"* There is the storytelling genre still abounding in the poems especially in *I Just Wanted her to be my Citizen*, and *Vessels of Dreams.* There is that scientific investigation and experimentation of art criticism interposing and being layered seam by seam with art mimesis. It directs the critic to this intersecting point, maybe as where the future of art criticism lies. You will find this experimentation in poems *To a Text Maker Who Leaves Nothing to Chance, Running towards the Song You Will Never Hear,* and especially in *Artist's Trails,* which I take as the crowning moment of this journey.

Experimentation and innovation abounds in the text, in form, in style, in content matter, the writer is a discoverer, every horizon is a life horizon. The poet deals with a broad subject matter, love in all its forms (*I Just Wanted her to be my Citizen, To, What it meant to her, What it meant to him, What really happened between them, Maita Shava)*, spirituality, and as I noted *Artists Trails* is the crowning poem, thus the spirituality in this book is individual, it's the artist's spiritual world. He is the prophet of his dreams, his world, his future, in the poem *There is You...*and in the poem *Running Towards the song I Will Never Hear,* he says,

> "I am the only thinker in my mind, always present, always willing to look.
> And if I don't, my art will be of no use, not even a hand without fingerprints is innocent."

There are poems that deal with the dreams/escapism and these poems gives the artistic edge to the collection, for instance, the titular poem, *When Escape Becomes the only Lover, Dreams, Body* (which straddles both the physical and the spiritual body), the pregnant otherness in *Walking, O Cheating Object! O Deathlessness! O Moon!,What it meant to her, What it meant to him...*

When Escape Becomes the only Lover is the last in this series, maybe in the future I will return back to the worlds of these 4 collections but I have moved onto the personal landscape of the artist in upcoming anthologies as the diary/journal has taken over.

But *When Escape Becomes the only Lover* is still relevant.We are living in an upheaval time with unending wars*A text for Baga, Is this the "next Rwanda?"*, with encroaching scarcity of resources, with the mother earth changing vastly due to global warming, thus human existence or life is really difficult and painful for a lot of us, and to deal with all these, to find the lover that really loves us, to find sanity, escapism is our only lover!

When escape becomes the only lover

When you have bagged pain inside like carrying knows no weight
And bled black you have, an uncommon white. And felt white you
have, an uncommon black
Escape becomes the only lover

Escape be-comes an artwork-in-progress
There is time to step away from the canvass, sometimes to canvass
into another room, sometimes to room into another canvass
The lover you have wanted to keep, sometimes onto the flowered
meadowlands, to hold her, and then…

To move away to Chinhoyi, to be a cave man, to curve in, in…

Transcending the oneness of being separate from others
Empty spaces, insane spaces, absences, like offering your own death
to death
Answers that are not on the wind

Escape becomes wide awake-dreaming, running away from you
On the path away from yourself, which is the only way to yourself
There are a few humans to be loved on the way; escape is a picker
that way
Escape chooses the wife you don't remember marrying.

Vessels of Dreams

And they leave the darkness in their own darkness. They unleave that place that is unnamed. They leave that being there. They unleave the unsaid, undone here. They leave some details, lost. They unleave memories that remained vivid and clear. They unleave their memories like a carry in arithmetic. They leave answers hidden in moonlight of memories. They leave the moon migrating to the south. They unleave the jazz of the sun. They leave the wind that carries waterless clouds. They leave footsteps that can never step. They unleave their footsteps in their sleep. They leave a thousand and one nights to dream. They unleave the source of so much reaching the other side of this night. They leave quite views of places left and paths imagined. They leave the underground railroads of their minds. They unleave the overground railroads of their hearts. They leave the road that seemed to twist and turn on its way to an African address. They unleave the bridge that has waited to connect them. They leave their boat on the mooring. They unleave their boat out at sea. They leave the font. They unleave the wishing well. They leave hours' flavours of silence. They unleave living in defiance. They leave the pink fresh scars of new mistakes. They unleave pimples of innocence. They unleave the aloneness of being separate from others. They leave the girls to become women so that they might return back to harvest wives. They unleave the crops of a drought year that they have now reaped. They leave maize stalks that were Indian summer scarlet and burgundy. They leave the bears of yesteryear to be with men they have cropped. They unleave the bear's soup can. They unleave

2

whatever that doesn't pretend. They leave rooms small enough to hold all of them as they prayed. They unleave the names of all those who have been washed downstream, interrogating God, "where the hell were you when our lives were hurt?" They unleave these prayers, needing separate rooms.

BODY

I am this nose; soft, big, fat, air gulping gluttony, gluttonous bolt of the door, door of the body. The eyes; hard, penetrating, soft, lazy, playful, sexy, pretty, conversing with this body, with me, with you, and with them..., them trees, over there. This hair; wavy, thick, Samson's long, dirty, thinning out, Zidane like, an over-used football pitch; there is a plateau coming off the kopje of this hill. Ears satellite dishes clotted with so much hearing, listening, information..., disinformation. I am these two, three, four, five, six, seven mouths (mouthhole, earholes, noseholes, skinholes, and other holes: wet clit, ass, dick...). A fireplace, dumpholes, toiletholes, heaven's womb, sizzling with sweetness, holes that gathers all over the heavy body (light body for you), are the souls, hearts, buried emotions, and love holes. These nipples; big tits, small tits, big Bobbies (B is in caps), huge rake, water melons, big jags, small oranges, dairy cow, flat man's lumps, hey what's happening there! It is an exploration of the body, always dependent and yet in constant control. This navel so full, small pack, Germany tanker, uterus, intestines loose, dislodged, gut inadhereble, bladder, liver, heart me, lungs, pipes, piles, bile, stones, ribs, backbone, bones, shit, food, garbage. Thinking of my body out of my body, its excesses: pus, urine, fart, saliva, poop, sweat, mucus. Body constrained, body on the drift, ambivalent. These legs, thighs, hips don't lie, feet, foot. He doesn't know that he is a spectre of himself, knees, joints, points, sores, dying in the waiting. Body not accounted for, body dead in this transfer of body to image. Malsain, rotted, dross, skeleton, snot, lichen, tomb, everything is my ghosts!

4

I Just Wanted Her to be my Citizen

I text her, good morning, I like you; you are special, flirting in codes.
She is beautiful, funny, fun, flawed, crazy, guarded, beautiful, beautiful, beautiful...
I text her again at night:
I like you; you are a great girl, sleep tight, un-breaking the codes in which we flirt.
She texts back; sleep tight, too.

I want her to be my citizen, the first citizen of my country.
She is beautiful, funny, fun, flawed, crazy, guarded, beautiful, funny, fun, crazy, guarded, beautiful...
Isn't love always about crossing back toward the other's shadows?

And what I now remember is how we stood in the warm pickle of the afternoon sun flirtingly holding each other, and for that brief moment we were poetry, standing in wonder, drinking the music in each other's eyes, body, minds, hearts...
How I felt the back of her head leaning into my arms as if she was drifting into sleep.

Our love was as natural as grass, leaves, dross and the dirty soil.
Our love was clean, balmy and pure like spring water.
Our love was warm, supple and solid like the human skin.
Our love was...,
... LOVE!

While romance was being cleaned, sent out, sipped out, shaken off, taken in, struck off, hold in, spoken off; purified by the hygiene of love- the formless human thing between us every morning was a person, a home.

Let's buy you new panties. What size are you?

Verdana font 12, lushly full, beautiful, funny, fun, flawed, crazy...

Guarded!

Always insane with something more potent than grief, which started in my toes and another that started in my head; cruising, coursing, careening through my bone marrow, flesh, blood, water, entrails to crash at the midpoint, which always uncovers itself?

Every note rented nude and returned nude.

The village idiot compared the clitoral moon with brown sugar, but I embarrassed myself by calling the moon vestigial and a pleasure dome.

A Joey cleared for the landing but still circling my plane in her skies, enjoying, joyful, around and about until her sexual howls were like a train that wanted to leave the station platform while the crowd were still climbing aboard.

Welcome aboard passenger!

Until the stars had evaporated from her eyes!

She told me the bees were dying and me, I am hoping breath by last breath that the hives somehow will remain open for that one last bee that I am, to find home.

She later told me that honey bees were the first creature to fly to heaven before Eden gained its necessary fundament knowledge of human sin and life.

She also told me that when the bees can't smell their name (home, heaven, hives...) they get disoriented and can even die.

Am I you, you are me. I am you, are you me, are you me....
I can even feel you in the texture of my waking dreams.
My body is repeating your code wearing your code, your story is repeating my code wearing your code, your body is repeating my code wearing my code, my story is repeating your code wearing my code.

My body is repeating your code...

If I write this letter of your body's code all over myself, how will I know where to start, with what? What is you, what is me, and how will I ever find the ending, the middle, the beginning...

Running Towards the Song I Will Never Hear.

I am the only eye above the painting
Running towards the colours I will never see.
Striving for the impersonal touch, like kitchen wall paper.
I am the only thinker in my mind, always present, always willing to look.
And if I don't, my art will be of no use, not even a hand without fingerprints is innocent.
And they shrug off, saying, "It's only a play, it's only a book, a radio show, a sketch, a poem..."
That is their safety net.

Not knowing it is reality, illusion, fantasy, truth...
I have weaved together in this poem thing.

Art is like running away from home on a way to home.
Running towards a song you will never hear.
The song's music, in my heart strings, is too fine to be in tune with the universe.
Transcends the aloneness of being in this moment, in this universe.
I would return to the world with new awareness about how to make it what I want it to be.

My work, my wounds, my warnings, my art
Surfaces plainly from the boils and lesions of sleep
I am the artist among the wounded (knee),
A poet made of work, thoughts and patience.

Through these tortured hands, mind, legs, heart, eyes,
The artist in me holds me in his bosom.
I paint, draw, write…, without licence.
I am an amateur.

And it's only the squares that are bothered.
The rest of us get on with the program.
Writing, drawing, painting, photographing, singing, and dancing together...
Fantasy and reality, truth and falsity, all acting upon the other.

We are victims of footsteps made over a lifetime.
Some may have been necessary at one point in life,
But the question I ask with my art is;
Are they appropriate to my life, to your life, to your situation?
Although the truth about this is always simple, It is not necessarily rational- it maybe a mystery.

Our personal thoughts determine how we respond to events in our lives. The situations have no good or bad quality in themselves. This reality is complex, but truthful, maybe beautiful.
Simple and beautiful.
Like the truth, itself.

Thus I draw what I feel, not exactly what I see.
I record the truth as it affects me.
The action itself is produced by my imprints: The way I am myself in this creation of my past, present, and future.
With words, actions, thoughts, feelings.

It's me who has the ability to change them.

Science, mathematics, business measures things,
The world, entities..., everything! Even you!
Insert tools between reality and our perceptions of the reality.
Our sense organs mediate between reality and self, our "self."
This reality is multilayered
This truth is not always on the surface.

Art is not necessarily the way things are arranged beautifully
But the ability to face the subject head on.
I act as a pupil of the truth, pulling it from wherever, from whatever
wields it.
I take the small slice of the visible world
Architect a plausible alternative.
Naming that thing that others attempt to keep silent about
My art is erosion, always moving away from what was meant.

Someone carries a broken guitar to my waiting hands.
I have to go on and strum the invisible strings
In my heart, on this guitar.
Not questioning the music I am making.

You have handed the guitar to me by reading me here
So listen to the song, close your eyes, open your eyes…
Open your ears, open your heart, open your mind…
Listen to the music bubbling in your ears,
Running towards the song you will never hear.

Art is a safe place to try to connect
Seemingly disparate opposites.
It is like two dance partners who fear each other as they yearn for
each other.
Art allows these contradictions (oh, so many in this poem now!)
To co-exist like dancing partners try to co-exist when they are not
dancing
By making sure that the music continues playing in their hearts.
They don't stop dancing to the music even when they have really
stopped.
They are dancing to the music in their hearts.

It reminds me of walking with a friend from the church. She loved
me, holding hands, unaware of our world, the gutted tarred roads,
dusty paths, rubbish, flowers... A girl I loved; we loved each other, as
friends, as brother and sister, as comfortable lovers, as partners. The
pole would come between us, we would separate hands, stop holding
each other. I felt so lost when I had to let go her hand, only to rejoin
hands beyond the pole. It was like loss of heaven when we had to
part hands.
Out of the loss from that pole, comes art.

Our hands were the objects
Objects I use, to join together, to create an art object.
These objects I link together get lost, separates.
Yet I do not stop from searching for new objects
Put them together, even temporarily.
I use these objects as scaffold for my art.

Being an artist is a licence to be myself,
It's the price to be myself.
That you will be yourself.
A lot of people cannot be themselves.
They can only do it through me, my art.

The idea to reveal it is not a light bulb turning on, but one turning off
to cast the reader, the audience, the viewer, the follower, you, him,
her; into a state of turmoil, contemplations, wonder, mystery…, the
mystic power; that rests within the music (languages, colours,
energies, meanings…) of my words, drawings, paints, photos, etc…
I bring it out, I create it, I manifest great power through it...
I am grateful
Grateful for the gift of life
The hallmark of the mystic,
The source of art, the primary wellspring of every belief system.

My art springs from the inner roots of the tree of the mind.
Sometimes from the internal emptiness of thought
Always figuring how far I can go without crossing the boundary.
Yes, that yellow line, there.
How that line can be pushed
To lose its function of limiting myself.

I am the bird sitting on a tree
Never afraid of the branch breaking
I am the bird sitting on top of electricity lines
Never afraid of electrocution
My trust is not on the branch

Not in the energy of the wires
My trust is in the blood in my legs
My trust is in the flight in my wings.

O Cheating Object! O Deathlessness! O Moon!

And there is still a vein of evening licking downwards from the yellow hole in the sky.

The pale force of nature colouring the gardens of our dreams (with greys, greens, browns, purples, yellows, blues, oranges, reds...). In the soft sweepings of this light we ride out a full moon; together, we are on display, we are like pregnant summer, emolliated by the stalking shadows of our pasts, this moon's golden brilliance slowly pouring at our horizon, is an open eye

Listening to music!

Classic rock music that makes use of the moon, sun, river, mountains, sea, ocean, sky, and stars...and especially the moon, the moon, the moon...

Most of the times, we just listen, drifting with the songs, contemplating, sometimes...

We didn't realise how many moon songs were out there until we started grouping them like that. Songs

Moon songs!

They were far more necessary, maybe, probably, because they don't take much work. You look up and there it is

A glimmering spot, globe-like, or is it really the moon through the wrong end of the telescope. We hash out a chorus...

O cheating object! O deathlessness! O moon!

Expressing our awe at the magnificence and complexity of it, the world...
Yet the light still comes down this far, and with legs, it screams to the core of the earth
And then we sit back and wait for the royalties to roll in

And the clouds comes from the east, lightish ones, darkish ones, tumbling over each other, making love in the eastern skies, some clouds blushing like the creamy goblets of sour milk. Kids eat it up, they think that's romance
Teens don't need the moon to tell them the name of what they are doing, right now
Names become less important than the activities that define them
Okay, you are an adult. I don't deny that! But, I can't teach you to adult.
You have a name, one that keeps the moon from rising on your fingernails. I won't use the moon on you, again
Yes, I have promised that!

Perspective is nothing more than the trick of the eye, a convergence of lines.
It's not music or memory or moonlight illuminating, the moon
No, I am not using the moon!
I am justsitting with it silently and letting it call my name in kind of ways
Calling my topsoil's soul!

The narration that punctuates (you say, "punctures") back to the narrowing bone

That our poetry might have the same turn on, each punctuated by a dramatic swoosh of the metaphors fighting allegories to describe the moon (I am sorry I have used it, again), allegories fighting images, images fighting iambics, iambics fighting conventions...

The sin of being visible
The winter moon pretends to see it all, to know it all

Okay, I will have to create my own moon. Not that giant spotlight shining down on you. I will paint mine and my mind will hang it in the skies, using my brushes to hang it up there.
The music in my eyes, is harpsichord wet!

I will start darkening it from one side, the dark moon punishing the arcing moon for my sins
My moon is not the bright one now
It is out of my reach
Your moon is out of reach

Oh, we went there as arrogant giants but came back petulant little shits.
There was no home for us there

But, we won't stop going there
And then we will make up and sort our differences under the soft shivers of the moon and mistake repetition for renewal, for solutions. We will confuse over-wear with trial and error; sorry, little holds us here.

O cheating object! O deathlessness! O moon!

Oh, I had promised you I would refuse to use this moon
A moon that tells us a tale, seducing us here, unafraid to continue...

Walking

Walking around something and walking around the same thing again, simply walking and stopping to talk, then walking, walking around the samething and walking around the same thing again, and again-simply walking and stopping to talk again...

Dogs pretend wolves, wolves pretend hyenas, hyenas pretend lions, lions pretend dogs, and the feeling is messy...

Walking...

To the Text Maker who leaves nothing to chance.

Touch, untouch me, lack of touch, there is a piece of you in such words, voices, the fertilization, float, sink, attach, wait, wait, wait... Touch, attach, untouch me, part precision, touch me, part poltergeist, untouch me, buzz the words, sink, float, the fertilization, there is brickwork behind the words, the lack of, the contact. Touching needs the part untouched, touch me...

Breathe, inhale, breathe, hold it in, breathe, exhale, we schlep and squeeze, like a baby all the words to each other, breathe... Breezy, warm, breathe, exhale, hold it in, only one word is left, this word... unword it, inhale, exhale, breathe... It's in the contrast that meaning forms.

Word it, unword it, words are erotic beings, blank parchment, silence, talking, quiet, let it enter, noise, talk, talk, talk..., you build a room like a wordless sentence. Stories, words, poems, voices, purpling with the winter, wording behind the radius of summer, listen, silence, listen, hear it..., and listen again.

To words negotiating with silence, with what can't be spoken, with what can be spoken, talk, silence... I want to hold, caress, read, imbibe, a black book full, empty it of screaming words, quiet words, quiet, quiet, quiet... Words need space to breathe; stories need what's left unsaid!

And to a text maker who leaves nothing to chance; change, unchange it…

To

To let this poem trot blindly the way youth and stupidity runs back
down the never ending source of remorse and genetics
To have glass shattering anger at this poem but
To still manage it until I finish writing it, you reading it
To let me skip to the past where grief gives way to a recurring dream
of finding whole other houses behind my mirror
And the bricks of my whole other houses were tears

To know that we will never know whether it is luck, strength,
blessing, curse or weakness to have survived where others could not
To know that suffering is like that too- five horizontal lines drawn in
pencil grounding the canvass of our life
To traverse that canvass, leaving black leaking spaces for air
To be untitled like everything else that takes too long to arrive
To be ill without falling ill

To think in a low voice so no one can see us
But no thought comes but only the wind
To be incapable of following our thoughts from one sentence to the
next one because the sentences breaks down and the gaps between
words become too long, too big for the words to connect, to hold
together

To feel guilty whilst trying to escape our own shadows
To feel guilty for walking away from our shadows and all the while
remaining behind
To be like a bazooka that hasn't lived up to its boom blast potential

To realize everything that I had declared buried, done with, is lying open to a second viewing

To know that she is going out with other boyfriends, she is on the prowl, whilst I am at home waiting, wilting, curving the darkness of my home with the chisel of my loneness
To storm abuse at my own reflection in the mirror
So that I might not feel this alone, so alone
To know of this loneliness so barren, is like my dried and shrunken testicles
I am dog-eared in many places it looks like I have a body
To feel the cold pain eating me from the centre of this body

To feel our suffering weighing more than what it weighed before we ever got here and what happens here weighs what it weighs
To live by burrowing in for we are people buried alive, and our tunnels seem strangely aimless, uprooted, gutted, fallen in….
To be a lorry tipper that vomits the sands and stones on our mind's tunnels
To know that children with deep eyes will be silent at the world just like old man with funny coughs
To be but a soul, formless, loitering around until emancipation
To burn each day, with more knowing, with more estrangement

To abandon misery until it becomes a mere concept, a poem
To leap with hungry aim
To be as ambitious as an argument
To run against the river

To question yourself about how to make it from one margin to another
To knit my heart back together every time I get up and it forgives me again and again
To move desperately towards meaning, where travelling becomes the basement of everything
To have an imagination fatefully embracing the birth of the world of appeal
To know that learning is life, that learning is the colour as life

There is You

There is where your eyes must be
There is that moment of meeting
There is a world of possibilities
There is where you have to start
There is where looking has to begin
There is a point, a place, a moment
There is you. You are there
Do you see it?

have we sounded the gong to announce our presence?
congratulations and decorations, at once!
boys and girls, please intake this phenomena
a thing in a thing, ladies and gentlemen-
it's something left unsaid, a thought still in the head
in and of itself

what we have seen is what the world acquires
from the strangeness of the way we see
have seen, what we have heard, hear-
mere echoes of ourselves, of others
sometimes, we speak: echoes, speech
so pure, almost unrecognizable, indecipherable,
and it's what we must wish for, for
no clutter, stripped bare, pure,
original, unswayable, colours
itself directly echoing in us

You are a moment, a place, a point
You are pointing us to you
You are full of possibilities
You meet yourself, you must be you
There is you. It is you.
Do you see it?

the worse part about looking at it for long
like looking at your chin whilst shaving it
is having to look at your face for far too long
staring at what has forgotten you
staring at the sight of lost breeze

that which is observed is a very wily,
mischievous, ruthless, insane, seer, seen (sin)
made up of eyes angling inwards (in)
willfully it produces the light by which it sees
everything that it does, says, thinks, feels
impacts, shapes, its soul
dents its world by, in itself

it's hard not to see the water
when looking at a fully flooded river
the river listening, seeing itself, flowing away
let the water's voice lead the river
and some days the river is enough
some days the river knows our names
and calls us.

Night Carrying Night

The curved sun of the night lounges
On the floor of heaven, in its western skirts
This sun that no longer shines
On all four corners of the earth
As night comes for a visit
Night carrying night in its brooding wings

There is exuberant growth of confused images all around me
Crackling geometric shapes, shaping up in the skies
Many more images obscure my lines of seeing
I delude myself more as I move into this delusion
This hidden world which I inhabit
Is invisible to those who are not a part of it
So, how good is good, what good is good, what a lie!
Complex things are always out in the open
And it's only what's simple that is always hidden, what a lie, again.

But every night my cricket visits me
Sings for me for several hours
Sad pretty music that sings with the dark
Music whispering in sign language into my soul
A tale of choices, of reflections, of faces, of coincidences
It's not so lonely, a story!

This night comes to me as one big continuous strand of night,
A waking world, the executioner of green thoughts

A magnetic field of wishful thinking
My thoughts escapes from me in the dark night skies
In little grey, greyish, darkish pieces,
I know I will never be able to change them back to green

There is memory of a man drinking
From the white basin where the sun prays,
Pays its respect, if he prays, tonight,
He prays that someone gives a soul
To cages that binds him in fear
That he would learn how to unlearn fear

He is in a room of things to lose
Outside stood fields of paths to chose
Ballsy as the blackbirds, but a pure sham,
An owl hoots its feathered fear,
Only darkness is its full stop
Whilst a foghorn booms bright light
In the dark night's mind, ruinous light

And a moon waltzing to the music of the blowing trees comes
The Zimbabwean moon is a waning smile, sky shy,
Singed against the velvet of the eastern skirts
Waxen and dermal is this moon's light
The moon spills and pours white light
On my sour night through the windows

This moon draws forth a wild mineral gleam on the windows
Holly with moon glow, with moonlight,

So charming, worth of magnetic truths
This moon houses the dead; I can see Michael Jackson's
Worn out, crackling face= faces
The moon whose pieces are my heart,
The past lost, the past falling back down

Pellucid in some luminescent candling
Some stars are floating in the mist of my thoughts, of a past life
Eyelids opened are stars, as the face of God, laughing mischievously
Warping net of omnipotent laughter
He is near crying, he is near laughing

Telling me of a hope that pricks my fingers and bleeds and bleeds
and bleeds
Even the most peeping sun will know that this sky is exhausted
Even the flight of a bat from the exhausted heat of the moon
As the moon licks the western skirts of the sky, half swallowed
I can't make this moon whole again. Sew it back together!

It's now at 2 AM, frogs confers on genius
Night falling away in embrace of dawn's yoke
I have my sure footed truth of
How I could only learn through my fears
As the years have, I feel more and more
Like an old man apologizing for stains left behind.
And I know I am getting too old to die young!

A text for Baga

115 000, 20 000, 11 000, 5 000, 2 000
115 000 refugees out of Nigeria
Carrying with them black barrels of sadness
20 000 refugees out of Baga
Carrying the distance from what they loved most
11 000 of the 20 000 left for Chad
5 000 found their way to just outside Baga
Carrying their grief into a hundredfold of grief
2 000 extirpated in Baga and Dolan Baga
My grief cannot translate this beyond words
I would have loved to fly, howl and sizzle
Instead of this meager mundane fizz

It felt like absence, it felt gone
2 000 wiped off the land, glutted, gutted, gunned
Like a loosening of the human sphincter
Into a river, an ocean of red blood flowing off
Bulleted blood pouring into Lake Chad
Vegetation, soils, ditches, stones, grass
Reddened; colored red by an insane painter
In the name of religion, this insane painter kills
Maim, detain, rape, and kill again, displace, without care
Leaving tapes of grief flowing, tapes and tapes of it,
Flowing out, all human shit flushed out at once!

3 700 razed structures in Baga and Doran Baga
By the madness that descended on 3 January 2015

And for 4 days this God killed, injured, displaced
Made us sick; we lost our families, properties, livelihoods
Using fear to make us conform to its teachings
This God has a name: **Boko Horam**

We have called out to it before
Asking it to bring back our girls it had abducted
And it brought them back strapping bombs on their little bodies
Burning us in its hot intelligence, fear and anger
Killing thousands all over our motherland
We have tried to stop calling for our babies back
Silently we have implored it, "Don't bring them back."
Not those ones who were coming back!

But the bullets never stopped flying our way
For the creation of a hard line Islamic state
In the north, north east Nigeria, it now controls
Killing over 2 000 in a small town!
This God killing civil vigilantes aiding the military?
This God doesn't care whom it would kill
And we can shout from our safe zones south
War crimes and crimes against humanity!
It doesn't bring them back, stop this killing God
The gulf between us sweeps breath across absence

A 50 year old running into the bushes
Dodging the red bullets, flying his way, says,
"I saw over 100 people being killed in Baga."
Another says, "Bodies were everywhere I looked."

Another says, "They were bodies decomposing in the streets."
Another stepped on dead bodies for over 5 kms
Another says, "Over 300 young woman were taken for amusements."
Another saw little children being gunned down
The pain of this powerlessness!

Half the body of the boy was out
Groaning red prayers
Breathing the hot angry smell of death
As bullets gutted it, pummeled it, and its mother
Killing a woman in labour, she died
With her unborn child
Death became the last word in human life
The last one in the shipwreck of humanity

It is all a cheap code
A God who kills to be worshipped
Doesn't care to kill itself; the unborn child
Who would worship it if it kills the innocent?
Who would be left in this killing field?
To worship it, to give alms to it, for it.
Who would care to love such a God?

My own maps are useless and invisible
This poem's inability to say what I want it to say
Your own editing of this draft of grief
A death without an echo, it means nothing
I am afraid to fall in love with this sound
The sound that can't be quieted

Of my own tears and their shapes
Yet we can only harmonize together in our soft
Braided chorus that sings of an ocean of grief

It takes hell

The tongue is the edge of a javelin
That can't be thrown far away
From the body

If it were only possible to stop with this
To hold off from the tens
Of thousands of words
As if they were just these few words

He wonders what words can do in the face of bullets
Yet he needed these words more than he needed life
His pen as mightier as, more potent than any sword
What of *against the bombs*, he doesn't know?

Everyday, the poet unfurls and braids words
Out of his dark inkpots
Truths torn from seasons
On the restless strand between sea and shore

He digs out the sugared-clothes of language,
Wrap them with the blood-drops of conscience,
Like cold cheese pieces

Most nights he stumbles on his own words
Does not have strength to make up a story
Lost in the content, in the thoughts, in judging
He is afraid of overusing a word

Like natural resources
Or even to shave his hairs, his chin, his head

The more the time passes by
The more his influence reaches
The tumultuous humanity's confluence
The poet, galloping with his own words

Can a poem flow through blue notes?
On a saxophone in some starless night of the mind

Oh yeh, it takes hell
To write a poem
Where poets pray like orgasm

It is a cheat code

She has plumb run out, up and up…
Up, up, up, up…
Is the only way to measure a year, a house
Unbuilding itself, in construction of the dead.
God's blazing fingers cryptically etched
On your mother's face

No one is there for you to impress upon now,
Except a drying mother, dying
Your mom- there, in the basement of your memories,
In a dark place, in the middle of a breath, where
It feels like it has stopped for a second.
half prayer, half request, half a whisper.
But no sound escapes you, encases you.

Howsoever long you now choose to stay here,
You need no keys, no locks
No door is locked, none is opened,
Every window is opened, every window is closed.
You have become the false bottom you had always hoped
You will touch if you burrow a little deeper.
Loss like this percolates underneath

Upto the point you want everyone you know to know of this
Yet you do not know who to let know of this
Angular the pain, diagonal the circumference synapses
Not communicating laughter, but a cry thing

Strapped inside your chest.

She tells you of her mother's marriage to the man who adored her
Not the man she doesn't mention when she mentions of her.
She tells you the best way to deal with this is to go through it
With faith, with the support of
Mourners who allow the mourner to mourn.
But do you tell her that from its case,
Your heart has vanished, a display now empty,
As empty as a vacant apartment, in a vacant street.

The point she tells you that part of
Mourning is helping other mourners respond to the mourner,
And you say when others lose sight of the mourner
All you will be left with is this-
A dying canary so bent and alone,
Wimping, singing, the morning off.
Let the bird's song sink into your skin
For this awhile you sing ice cold tears.

But when the stars burn,
The songs from their mouth is dark
As if they have stretched thin as wilted tissue.
The wind will not your friend;
You don't concentrate on the trees,
But follow deep blue black skies

What it meant to her

Her name is Eve, a folly of a name
She carries it as if she has just found it
On the sides of the roads he never walked
She is a wolf, he is a werewolf
She chooses him, for him: Adam
The wicked, the misfit, the imperfect

She likes holding things in.
She has these colours and they wake
When she nestles with a man,
To hold him in, in that way, someday
Her voice slips through the open windows
Turns the streets into honey

To fool invaders,
Is how it felt when she kissed him?
Like out of order streets signs, rearrangement
She kept checking the pantry of their marriage,
Has enough been stowed away, is there enough to last
The bridges she has burned down, at what cost?

She thought she would really be able to take on the slaughtering
werewolf,
Rotting seeds, but the stars made her feel guilty when she couldn't
Only rotting apples kept falling into her welcoming hands,
She couldn't keep a few
She washed bed sheets with her tears

She watched her love dying from boredom,
Sleeping in the sour boredom smelling blankets

The difference between hunting for food and hunting
For the fun of it, is one sandwich less for breakfast
Half doubt, half believe, nothing will hurt her anymore
She really wants to tell him she only loved his shadows

She is still at the age where she bears her new breasts
Like pert little deities seeking rightful homage
She can see the look in her new boyfriend's eyes
As she pulls out his heart- the pure, terrible trust
Of someone who knows her
Someone who wants to give her what she wants

The voyage across her breasts reminds her to breath
As she turns on his faucet
The dark roar of a September storm!
Later that year they reached the moon
And they even landed on it.

What it meant to him

Does he mistake the warning thunder in his heart?
Could it be desire, a call, a void, a covert?
He sees him and her tattooed around the curving arm
She is a wolf, and he thinks, "I am a werewolf"
It was him who begged and begged, threatened
And allowed himself to chain himself to her side,
Close to his heartbeat as a watch,
That he might, oh, he doesn't know what!

She was a wolf, he was a werewolf
Because of this habit of his of staring into eyes
What big eyes she had, he saw, as,
A hunger pang hit him hard;
He could nearly taste his own backbone
So, the better to devour her whole!

Mouths moving towards the reply of her eye,
He likes the first kisses, the melting part
Woman's kisses, ephemeral, vanishing
The touch of her tongue, feet, fingers, body,
The acquiescence of his ears, heart, mind and soul
Climax comes to them as a conniption fit

He loved her more than the worms aspired to love her
And he felt that if he loved her enough.
Time would allow itself to be texted into slowing down

But desire wade to the shore in tatters, in love lost
Any word from her withered like a severed limb
The honey in her voice sickened him

Now he really wants to tell her he only loved her eyes
As he remembers why he loved her
Before they were both washed out
He is now a Fat Cat Adam
A perfidious Adam as disrupter of Eden
Of the modern marriage that unravels in
Divorces on the pages of this poem

Like a painting of roses and tears
In the guidebooks on recovery
For him forgiveness comes naked,
Adorned with evidence of a long difficult journey
He is his bitter sweet unmanageable creature
Uses love as an eraser, doodles on misspellings
In the deepest night, they whisper their stories

Boy to boy, he kisses him harder
Sweet hocked swine's heart,
His love, a swain's love-
A swansong, the sun of his life!
His boyfriend is Sexica,
S(he) collects bits of life
That s(he) dares to return

What really happened between them

They are wolves among us,
They are brutal,
Licentious, cowed, sly, fierce, penned,
They are dampened by circumstances,
Famished, ravening,
They are whipped to furies by blood,
Primed for attack

And it happens that which happens
When a need is too big
For the theory that feeds on it?
It was a war of different loves
A war between things that makes us human
Love, like death is a wolf, is a werewolf

Two people can light the map entirely
Bleed mouthfuls of rich decadent love
Into a thick skinned vision, flat and whitened
But the love clock that we arrive in
Might be too green and too thin
To fit almost everyone

We wonder if we can manufacture love in a relationship,
If we brace up to it with curiosity and boredom
Construct girlfriends; construct boyfriends, construct love,
Stabilizing a building only meant to be temporary.
What is love?

Brilliant white vestments and paper bondages?
No regrets!

Love with walls, lines and rules, love build on an epicenter
And if the diameter of a love song is longer than the melody of its
existence,
Will the song remain unresolved?
Do we know why we want to colonize another girl, or boy…
When there is a lot of empty land within the one we have
We haven't traversed?

There were many miles of bleak terrain between them
A lot left undone, unknown, untouched, untorched

We can arrange to meet others and lose ourselves along the way
To come to know others in so far as we ignore ourselves

What is love?
That doesn't say *good morning*,
I love you,
Not a wink or a purr or a touch-
Withholding. Still

Maita Shava

Mhofu yomukono, Ziwewera
Hekani mutekedza
Vakatekedzana pa Janga
Wakapiwa mukadzi munyika yevaNjanja
Hekani mutekedza, vari muhera mukonde
Zwaitwa mhukahuru vemiswe inochenga muviri

Ah, ko mazwi angu angapinda sei muninga yepfungwa dzenyu?
Ndingataure   here   kubudikidza   nemi,   muromo   wangu
urikukwakukakwakuka, mwoyo wenyu wanyorovera
Munogona kundiudza zvose, Shava
Nhasi, ndichaedza kutaura nomunemi
Iyi inyaya yenyu iyi, Shava
Ndononamata kusarasa ngano yenyu iyi

Ndakakusarudza iwe nokuda kwako chete
Uri munamato wangu wakahwandiswa
Uri ngirozi iri munzira iri pakati pepasi nedenga
Tirikuenda kunyika itsva pamwechete

Paivapo pataisangana, tichinwa, kuseka, kutsvodana
Zvinyamubhesese   zvichitikurudzira   nezvidimbu   zvemimhanzi
yenziyo dzatairangaridzwa
Tsvodo? Nganiko? ah, handingakuudzei
Ndakakugumbatira nguva refu zvangu pawaiva wati raremangwana
Muromo wangu unenzara yokuda kukuswada mandiri.
Zvishomanana tsvoda dzichinanga pamurumo pako

43

Mune ramangwana ngwanani, ndokunyorera *wamukasei* tichisasana zvechihwandehwande hedu
Dimwe nguva, ndaisatomboziva zvandaitaura zvangu

Zvikwawu zvandakatsetsa kubva mumakodo kuitira rudo rwako
Mwoyo wakapetunura mwoyo wangu
Kuitira tsanga yembeu yomwoyo wangu
Irikumerera muvhu rako, muti wangu munyoronyoro
Ivhu remaruva angu anoyevedza kudairira nziyo yorudo rwako
Uri furafura rangu rinonwa kubva muhana nhete yemaruva angu

Uri patya rangu romuninga dzepfungwa dzangu, diziro remapapiro angu atyoka
Kunge shiri mbiri dzehurekure, tamhara pabango regore rokudenga
Tichanyora nomwoyo yedu yasunganiswa paganda regore iri
Mumvuramvura nohuhwandi hwemvura yemakore tichakura pamwechete
Nhasi ndonokupai mwoyo wangu nekiyi yeninga dzepfungwa dzangu
Semubikiro wezvinonaka, Shava
Rudo rwako rwunondizadza nemufaro nemanyemwe sehari dzezvinotapira
dziri muninga yenyikadzimu chisionekwi.
Ndawuwudza halleluiah, Ndawuwudza halleluiah, Ndawuwudza halleluiah.
Ndinokudai Shava, Ndinokudai Mhofu, Ndinokudai Ziwewera.

Thank you Shava

The Great Eland bull. The Runaway
Thank you very much. The one who carries heavy loads
Those who challenged each other at Janga
Those who were given wives in the country of the Njanja people
Thank you my dear mutekedza, those in uHera Mukonde
It has been done Great Animal, those with tails that are intimate with body

Oh, how can one person's words enter the soul of another?
Can I speak through you, my mouth keeps moving, your heart is still
You can tell me anything, Shava
Now, I try to speak through you
This is your story, Shava
I pray never to lose your story

I chose you for you
You are my hidden prayer
A saint as a point of moving from earth to heaven
Herding for a new country together

There was a rendezvous, a drink, a laugh, a kiss
Hummingbirds motivating us to sound snatches of remembered songs
A kiss? How many? Oh, I couldn't say
Holding you longer each time we say goodnight
My mouth hungering to take you in
Slowly moving each kiss closer to your mouth

In the morning I would text you *goodmorning* and flirt in codes
Sometimes, I didn't know what I was saying

The oars I carved out of my bones for the love of you
The heart that opened my heart
For the wheat of my heart
Sprouting in your soil, the plant of my tenderness
The soil where my roses blooms to the tune of your love
You are my butterfly drinking from the soft heart of my roses

You are the twin of my soul, a sanctuary of my broken wings
Like two swallow birds, we have landed on an arm of a heavenly cloud
And engraved our joined souls on the cloud's skins
In the balmy and bounty of the cloud's rains we will grow old together
Today, I present my heart and the keys of my soul to you
As a dish of delight, Shava
Your love overwhelms me with ecstasy like clay pots of sweetened drinks
In the cave of the mystery of myth
I chant halleluiah, I chant halleluiah, I chant halleluiah
I love you Shava, I love you Great Bull, I love you The Runaway

Is this the "next Rwanda?"

Helicopters hovering\ roving\ round\ around\ loitering hooligans.
Burning streets/ humming/ singing/ smoking/ angry... choruses
into the air
People being raped\ touched\ tortured\ hacked\ forced\
disappearing...
Children gutted, ----------- ------------ beheaded; an oblation to
machetes, AK47s, bombs, pangas, & chainsaws of destruction...
6,000 to 10,000 boys & girls ...tots, totting, toy-
toying
Forming part of these armed groups belonging,
owning:::::: it
Fanatics stampeding| stamping on| a civilian youth on the head|
stabbing him| stoning him... stones raining down on his soft soil:
gorging it| raining| rain raining| rivulets of red water| watering| the
hard soil
His body is dragged raggedly through the streets. O,
bringing back medieval France!
Soldiers look on @ this action movie; Jason Stratham,
transport me a tale! For this poem fails me;;;;;;;;
& then dismembers me..... burned... **d....**

This war is a kind of a.... ▱building in which the children asks
when shall love, love/ love/ love/ love me.... arrive @
the front door
And in another month, about **1,000** people are killed. I said,,,,,,,
killed!
Killed| killed\ killed/ killed| killed\ killed/ killed.....

47

This war is now a   beer hall in which adults (AU, UN, EU,
the fighters, men, woman, you, and you, and you…) ask whether
there is enough liquor   in the pantry to ensure victory. Me, too!
Functioning on the territory of this squalid nation
                         Is a presidency without law, functioning
police   & courts?
Surely the other shoe will have to fall; falling   falling   falling
falling

The Séléka/ lekker north east/ rebels/ rebelling/ grouping/
regrouping/coup-ing/whooping/   for reprisal attacks\
attacking\ Anti-balaka\ unlucky\ rebels\ Christians
Anti-balaka/ barraging/ rampaging/ killing Séléka   rebels
&   Muslims
Muslims   Vs.   Christians
in   Muslim areas.
Consumed by the doing/ doing/ doing/ doing…..   not by
its meaning,
Christians   Vs.   Muslims
in   Christian areas.
The chaos in this landscape is complimented with harsh particulars:
Muslims cannibalizing Christians, Christians cannibalizing Muslims!
Bringing us to the discombobulated perception of our surroundings
In this dangerous hour of forgetting, let us be careful of the noise,
which is rising to attack us with a lack of temperance
Let us not be seduced by the seraphim of more-
Unexplainable events!
Are their gold standards
            Pushing history through space

In time we shall all return

The theory holds, tight as an atom
Is   this   the   "next
Rwanda?"

Bosnian
Genocide's aftermath may be more apt
People   are   moving
into religiously cleansed neighbourhoods.
Mixed in the permanence of blood,
dirty and dusty
The sound wearing wind in its teeth is
Partitioning the Central African Republic into separate
Christian and Muslim states

By May   **2014,**   it was reported
around   600,000
Were   internally   displaced,   with
160,000
In the capital, Bangui/ Bangui/ Bangui/ Bangui…. I cry for you….
physique ruthless, a territory theory!
The Muslim population of Bangui has dropped from   **138,000**
to   900.
And a food crisis is looming! ♀

This Bangui shows me her new earrings| lipstick| jewelry|
fashionable clothing-
That distract/ detract/ intract/-able,   from the
scars/scaring/ her cheeks

49

Revealing our paths\ roads\ bridges\ stations\   to ourselves
&   how to burn them down
No one knows for sure when Africa will actually   leave/
depart/ arrive/ stay///////
Herding for a new beginning we are forced to ponder| listen|
watch| not   arrive:::::

Always making excuses
                              It   feels   natural,
soothing like home
              A home where time hammers us into a place!

Artist's Trails

Signs that name objects speak about themselves but do not put the objects into words. When questions, I mean objects, cannot be put into words, when the words to search for the answers, I mean signs, are not actually words, the answers cannot be put into words, words cannot manifest into things, words manifests to themselves.

This Words Tower works its wounds for warnings, it says: In this Words Babel, no one is excluded from the knowledge of the roundness (life) of things, whether dead or alive. Life as a school; why not try to take its curriculum. The first lesson is on human touch, and the experiment is: Microwave your pride!

Here are the results:

Take advantage of the ever-changing point.
Unlike the fixed point where you can huff and puff locating it with your body, the ever-changing point requires the outside-the-body presence. Some might call that a soul, psyche, consciousness, conscience, spirit, *mweya*...
Just locate it!

Allow it to keep changing in the space. Add circular lines around its change fields. Lines that touch these ever-changing *change* points will together become your construction block. Set (put), what others might refer to as input and unset (unput) yourself between these construction blocks- gather yourself by inhabiting the emoticon theatre. Ask yourself, or just answer, "am I reversing the pattern of the physical body."

The art of finding the physical body does not support weight; rather it represents the weight-bearing emotions of human beings.
Then ask again, "am I reversing the pattern of the spiritual body"

This is an ordinary enough telling, this telling and this not telling of things. The kind of things anyone may find themselves living with or not telling when talking about things:
Living, so say you what say I, tell of this switchback of shadows, a new organ that grows in his heart.

We trace the shadows of it against the download of itself, chewing just people things... like that; *walk-away-from-your-shadow* play. The shadow swallows him and it is warm in the inside of him as it keeps him from sleeping. He had no idea it was a burden of all two-sided things, the burden of every wish. What wish?

The stars horizon is an empty line of music, he basks in the trance of this music, the folded stars of Cassiopeia's dream go down the grid, then up to the nearest bright moment, hip down, and another moment joint up, and then again and again. See, See it. The see-saw, the spin-whirly. *Hmmm*. We are listening to the subterranean lullabies of plate-shift shitting and ordaining the extinction of us.

Selfish is neither sell nor fish. Marita was arrested for pretending to be in a marginal box, an imaginary box. Maryam was hospitalized in a nut house for impersonating longing, okay just attempting to sit on its thighs. Lazarus was jailed for trying to disintegrate himself- he now prays for small things. He now prays to the God of Small Things. I didn't say to the small god, a Buddha! Let this be victory enough, the echoes of us being in our heads against us.

Where are we without this, what are we without this, this is a revision, a beginning, a compromise, an improvisation- we will go our whole life for this and only and only, settling for something, anything, okay everything and then ex(im)ploding. I have made it a word! Feel it smash, shave and smooth away our directional mistakes.
We all owe rent!

Artist's Trails, frozen echoes, pure impressions of the truth! This is now where ideology criticism meets memes. We could give this language a heart. Keep talking; telling, talking: we can see it moves things. Half-half, Ho-hum. This language map.

He is just an average pen, going his normal routines, scribbling nonsense on paper with this black, blue, red…, ink; there is nothing to see here.
Vanquish the script!
Come back!

Publisher's List

If you have enjoyed *When Escape Becomes the only Lover*, consider these other fine books from Mwanaka Media and Publishing:

Cultural Hybridity and Fixity by Andrew Nyongesa
The Water Cycle by Andrew Nyongesa
Tintinnabulation of Literary Theory by Andrew Nyongesa
I Threw a Star in a Wine Glass by Fethi Sassi
South Africa and United Nations Peacekeeping Offensive Operations by Antonio Garcia
Africanization and Americanization Anthology Volume 1, Searching for Interracial, Interstitial, Intersectional and Interstates Meeting Spaces, Africa Vs North America by Tendai R Mwanaka
A Conversation…, A Contact by Tendai Rinos Mwanaka
A Dark Energy by Tendai Rinos Mwanaka
Africa, UK and Ireland: Writing Politics and Knowledge Production Vol 1 by Tendai R Mwanaka
Best New African Poets 2017 Anthology by Tendai R Mwanaka and Daniel Da Purificacao
Keys in the River: New and Collected Stories by Tendai Rinos Mwanaka
Logbook Written by a Drifter by Tendai Rinos Mwanaka
Mad Bob Republic: Bloodlines, Bile and Crying Child by Tendai Rinos Mwanaka
How The Twins Grew Up/Makurire Akaita Mapatya by Milutin Djurickovic and Tendai Rinos Mwanaka
Writing Language, Culture and Development, Africa Vs Asia Vol 1 by Tendai R Mwanaka, Wanjohi wa Makokha and Upal Deb

Zimbolicious Poetry Vol 1 by Tendai R Mwanaka and Edward Dzonze

Zimbolicious: An Anthology of Zimbabwean Literature and Arts, Vol 3 by Tendai Mwanaka

Under The Steel Yoke by Jabulani Mzinyathi

A Case of Love and Hate by Chenjerai Mhondera

Epochs of Morning Light by Elena Botts

Fly in a Beehive by Thato Tshukudu

Bounding for Light by Richard Mbuthia

White Man Walking byJohn Eppel

A Cat and Mouse Affair by Bruno Shora

Sentiments by Jackson Matimba

Best New African Poets 2018 Anthology by Tendai R Mwanaka and Nsah Mala

Drawing Without Licence by Tendai R Mwanaka

Writing Grandmothers/Escribiendo sobre nuestras raíces:Africa Vs Latin America Vol 2 by Tendai R Mwanaka and Felix Rodriguez

The Scholarship Girl by Abigail George

Words That Matter by Gerry Sikazwe

The Gods Sleep Through It by Wonder Guchu

The Ungendered by Delia Watterson

The Big Noise and Other Noises by Christopher Kudyahakudadirwe

Tiny Human Protection Agency by Megan Landman

Soon to be released

Ghetto Symphony by Mandla Mavolwane

Of Bloom Smoke by Abigail George

Sky for a Foreign Bird by Fethi Sassi

Denga reshiri yokunze kwenyika by Fethi Sassi

A Portrait of Defiance by Tendai Rinos Mwanaka

Where I Belong, moments, mist and song by Smeetha Bhoumik

Nationalism: (Mis)Understanding   Donald Trump's Capitalism, Racism, Global Politics, International Trade and Media Wars, Africa Vs North America Vol 2 by Tendai R Mwanaka

Ashes by Ken Weene and Umar O. Abdul

Ouafa and the Thawra: About a Lover From Tunisia by Arturo Desimone

Thoughts Hunt The Loves/Pfungwa dzinovhima Vadiwa by Jeton Kelmendi

https://facebook.com/MwanakaMediaAndPublishing/

Printed in the United States
By Bookmasters